"Writer and mi~~~~~, ~~~~ Casey, in *Get Personal*, reminds us of something that is lacking in the Church today—the transformation that happens when we share our own vulnerable stories. In this little book, you'll find a huge, worthy message—sharing our faith stories shows us that we have a place in God's epic story of the universe. Your story matters. The telling of it matters. The sharing of it matters. And Casey, a gifted writer used to sharing stories, gives her readers great advice about how to recognize and tell their own. A great tool for those looking for a personal way to impact their neighborhoods and communities."

LAURA ANDERSON KURK
author of *Glass Girl* and *Perfect Glass*

"The stories we have through Christ are gifts to be shared both with seekers and with other Christians. In *Get Personal*, Erin Casey helps us uncover our stories and recognize the ways God still works in our lives to reveal His grace and mercy. Read it, work through the exercises, and then share your story. Acknowledging Him and sharing what He's done, changes our lives and relationships at a heart level."

ALLYSON LEWIS
author, speaker, and time-management expert

"*Get Personal* is an absolute must for those thinking about sharing their story. Author Erin Casey passionately demonstrates how to move your personal testimony from neutral to drive. Get engaged... share your story. You'll want to buy a copy for yourself and several for your friends and ministry partners."

JAN COATES
Christian speaker and
author of *Set Free* and *Attitude-inize*

"Erin Casey's book, *Get Personal*, issues forth a call to believers to join the Great Commission in a non-threatening way... even in our world of political correctness. She helps us grasp the fact that our simple stories, the ones we think of as common everyday stuff, can be transformed into powerful, life-changing encounters when we find the courage to share with others. She helps us clarify which stories to share, how to simplify them, and talk of them in a non-religious way. It's easy to see how we, as the Church, could change the world one story at a time by following the guidance in this book. *Get Personal* is a much-needed tool for the Church today."

DEBY DEARMAN
worship and arts pioneer and
co-writer of the song "We Bring the Sacrifice of Praise"

"We all love stories... telling them *and* hearing them. I love that Erin 'gets' this! In today's multicultural society, you don't have to leave home to make disciples of 'all nations.' And as Erin Casey writes, 'You can be considerate someone's worldview without wavering on your own.' It all begins by telling your personal, authentic stories. In my case... with a drawl, at a high speed, and very animated, but my story, just the same."

CARRIE WILKERSON
author of *The Barefoot Executive*

"For someone who has not yet meet Jesus, our stories could be the closest thing to the inside of a church that person has ever known. Through our own words of truth, forgiveness, healing, and redemption, others can see the gift and benefit of freedom that is available through Christ's love. In *Get Personal*, Erin Casey explains why it's important to share your story, gives you the ideas and steps to do it, and offers sound advice for making it relatable and relevant. This is a wonderful read and how-to guide for ministry, Bible study, and faith-in-the-marketplace groups."

JOEL BOGGESS
radio host and author of *Finding Your Voice*

"You don't have to change people's lives—Jesus will do that—but you do have to set the stage for Him by telling other people your story. In *Get Personal*, Erin Casey gives us all a confidence and a strategy for how to comfortably share our faith stories with others. Read this book and watch how its principles transform the lives of the people closest to you!"

RORY VADEN
co-founder of Southwestern Consulting™ and
New York Times bestselling author of *Take the Stairs*

Get Personal

Get Personal

the importance

of sharing your

faith story

Erin K. Casey

Get Personal: The Importance of Sharing Your Faith Story
© 2014 by Erin K. Casey

Cover Design: Genesis Kohler
Copy Editors: Brian Casey and Diane Krause

This book is available at special discounts when purchased in quantity for use as premiums, promotions, fundraising and educational use. For inquiries and details, visit ShareYourFaithstory.net/get-personal/group-study-discount/.

Published by Gypsy Heart Press
ISBN 13 TP: 978-0-9832514-7-7
ISBN 13 Ebook: 978-0-9832514-8-4
Library of Congress Control Number: 2014908210

For Worldwide Distribution, Printed in the U.S.A.

Contents

Foreword

I have always loved the stories of the Bible. When asked a challenging question, Jesus would launch into an interesting story. Want to understand the healing power of forgiveness? Let me tell you a story about a prodigal son. Need to know about the snowballing effect of habits? Listen to this story about sowing seeds.

With the given name of Daniel, I was fascinated by the story of the biblical Daniel and how he stood up for his beliefs, even to the point of being thrown into a den of lions. What a riveting way to absorb the value of being true to your convictions.

From the inspiring book you are reading now, you are going to learn how to increase your own ministry effectiveness by following Jesus's lead by telling stories. You'll learn how your stories of transformation can challenge, comfort, and encourage others — without teaching or preaching.

In my role as a coach and mentor, I find myself gravitating more and more to the use of stories in leading people to clarify their own life principles. In making a point about the choices we have, I often tell snippets of my own faith journey. For example, I explain that like anyone else, I can tell my life story as a healthy version or a victim version.

I can tell my story like this:

I grew up in a home where we didn't even have running water until I was in the eighth grade. I knew nothing but poverty. As a five-year-old, I was forced to get up at 5:30 a.m. to do my share of the farming chores. Most Christmases I got a new pair of blue jeans — my one pair for the coming year. I was not allowed to wear neckties or fancy clothes. Because of my parents' legalistic religious beliefs I was not allowed to go to movies, dances, or sporting events. Our home was rigid and somber with little laughter. I received zero in financial help for college from my parents. Both money and education were dangerous. I hated the cold weather in Ohio. If only I had been born into a family with more opportunity.

Or, I can tell it from another perspective:

In my family we learned how to make good use of everything – nothing was wasted. We grew our own food and I created toys from things other families discarded. As a small boy, I had the opportunity to experience real work and to begin my commitment to work that was meaningful and profitable. With no television or radio in our house, I became an avid reader, and reading opened me up to a wealth of wisdom and knowledge that still serves me well today. I worked right through my college years and valued the education I paid for myself. My father's devotion to his religious views prompted me to study deeply to formulate beliefs to which I could be equally committed. Today, I value the work ethic and the uncompromising integrity I learned in that strict Amish/Mennonite environment. As my own man, I wore neckties until I came to my own realization that there was more than legalism to provide reason for not wearing the silly things. The creativity and ingenuity I experienced as a child has served me in a thousand ways in helping me "see" opportunities others miss.

Both of those versions of my life are equally true. If you'd just met me, which of those stories would make you want to get to know me more? Which one do you think makes me more confident, happier, and gives me more energy today? The point is, the way we frame our stories shares with the world our values, beliefs, and perspectives.

In *Get Personal*, Erin walks us through an engaging process for sharing our faith through our stories. You'll enjoy the reminders of the great stories and truths from the Bible and how leaders of our faith have always used stories to move us forward in our commitment to a life of eternal significance. You'll also clarify your own faith as you grow in confidence with this effective method for challenging, encouraging, and inspiring others.

DAN MILLER
Life Coach and author of *48 Days to the Work You Love*
48Days.com

Introduction

The Kinks sang, "I'm a lover, not a fighter." Well, I'm a writer, not a talker.

Don't get me wrong, I love to talk with people. I can chat for hours. (Just ask my family how hard it is to get me in the car after worship service on Sunday morning.)

But when it comes to sharing my faith stories, I often feel a disconnect between the passion of my heart and the words that fall haphazardly out of my mouth. I know what I believe; I just don't always know how to say it. I am apt to stumble over my thoughts during a conversation with a person, and then after we've parted ways, my brain fills with all sorts of brilliant things I wish I'd said. Add in the self-inflicted stress that comes from my not wanting to botch opportunities to share something important—especially when it comes to matters of spiritual life and death—and too often, I either stand there tongue-tied or offer an incoherent message that confuses people instead of enlightening or encouraging them.

That's why I wrote this little book. I wanted to get better at telling my faith stories. I wanted to be able to have brief conversations that offered hope or sparked someone's desire to know more about the Jesus I love. And I wanted to do it without sounding preachy, religious, weird, or like a goody-two-shoes. I also wanted to encourage other Christians to speak up about Jesus and the difference knowing Him makes in their lives.

The Power of Stories

I've spent the past decade writing and editing stories. I know the power a well-crafted tale has to connect people to new ideas and products. There's a saying at the company where I began my writing career: *Facts tell, stories sell*. Salespeople have a tendency to throw loads of facts about a product's features at their prospects. And why not? It's easy to talk about costs, ingredients, components, manufacturing processes, or clinical studies. The unfortunate and unintended outcome of information overload is often a confused or overwhelmed pro-spective client. Instead of buying in, they zone out and ask for more time to make a decision. Then they add your literature to their to-read-much-later pile.

Dumping facts on people rarely persuades them to want to consider your company, your product, your service—or your God. In sales, a better tac-tic for helping someone understand your prod-uct or service's practical uses is to share how you or someone else has personally experienced and benefited from it. The same thing is often true in matters of faith. Though they may never verbalize the questions, what people really want to know is: "What's in it for me? How is this (product, service, or even faith) going to help me personally? Has it worked for you?"

Yes, of course, people need facts to make well-thought-out decisions. In business, you have to provide the specs and costs. And in matters of faith, people need to know the scriptures that explain the Good News of Jesus Christ and the reality of sin and death, Heaven and Hell. So share those! *Please*, open up your Bible and share its truths liberally! But consider, too, the value of putting the reality of the Word into the context of your life and sharing those stories as well.

Saved or searching, we all need to be reminded of God's interest in us individually and His love for us personally.

Jesus understood that stories have the power to help people connect the dots between His truths and their own lives. Rather than simply telling people what to do, He told parables that allowed them to see themselves in the story. We read those stories even now and identify with the prodigal son, or the one who stayed at home (Luke 15:11-32); as the hurting, needy person helped by a complete stranger (Luke 10: 25-37); or as the humble tax collector or perhaps the prideful Pharisee (Luke 18:9-14). Jesus's parables teach, comfort, and convict, often without a word of condemnation.

Beyond the parables, real-life accounts of sin and redemption experienced by individuals throughout the Bible reveal God's desire for people to know Him. Consider how He took ordinary men like David, Peter, and Saul/Paul, interrupted their lives, taught them, and loved them enough to both expose their sin and forgive them when they repented. How different are their stories from our own? Doesn't God still do the same for us today?

In the pages that follow, you'll read a few of the reasons I believe we must share our faith stories. You'll find some pointers on how to discover your stories, and share them effectively. And while sharing stories is an important part of evangelism, *Get Personal* is not a how-to book on evangelism or leading people to Christ. Rather, it's about sharing your life and your Saviour with others — Christians and seekers alike. Because I believe it's as important to talk with Christians about what God is doing today and how the Holy Spirit helps us navigate this treacherous world, as it is to talk with people who don't know Jesus yet. Saved or searching, we all need to be reminded of God's interest in us individually and His love for us personally.

Our faith stories offer present-day proof that God is alive and powerful, and that He still wants all people to know Him (2 Peter 3:9). It is encouraging to hear how someone came to know Jesus as their Saviour, or how God orchestrated a "God-incidence" that changed a person's heart or life. Let's not be guilty of snuffing out the light these stories offer by keeping them to ourselves. It's time to speak up, to get personal, and to share what matters most.

I look forward to hearing your story.

Everyone Has a Story

*I*n the film *Date Night*, Phil and Clare Foster (Steve Carell and Tina Fey) play the game, "What's Their Story?" In a hilarious (if off-color) sketch, they choose an unsuspecting couple and proceed to make up a story about them. I often do the same in my mind when I'm out shopping or riding on the train or bus. It's an exercise that challenges me to be observant and descriptive. Those moments of people-watching and weaving tales spark creativity. They also remind me that everyone has a story.

During the past ten years, I've helped hundreds of people tell their real-life stories. Some of those individuals have been celebrities and CEOs. Interviews with those folks typically require fewer questions because they've told their stories countless times. Even if they haven't intentionally rehearsed it, the requirement of retelling their stories for marketing purposes has forced them to think through how they got to the red carpet or the corner office.

Practice helps people polish their words and craft quotable sound bites. When I talk to a practiced interviewee, I listen to their packaged story, because it is important to know how they rose to the top (or fell from fame). But I don't stop there. I ask questions that move them away from the rote how-I-got-here story. I want to know what's going on *now*. What's next? And how do the changes or challenges they're facing make them feel? That's the story I want to tell. The challenge, the struggle, the joy, or the uncertainty reminds us that even people who seem larger than life are just as human as the rest of us.

Although my writing career has given me the opportunity to talk with A-listers and mega-millionaires, some of my favorite interviews have been with "regular" people — those who shy away from the spotlight and think of themselves as "normal." When asked to share their stories, the conversations often begin something like, "I don't know where to start," or "I don't think I have that much to say," or "I'm not really all that special or unique."

Their humility, though endearing, prevents them from understanding that their stories are powerful and invaluable to other "normal" people. It's difficult for most people to imagine themselves as the CEO of a Fortune 500 company or a movie star. But an everyday person? They're easy to relate to. They're like you and me. They're people who are "nothing special" but have learned or experienced something important—and their wisdom has the potential to benefit countless others... if only they'll share it.

The same scenarios hold true for our Christian stories; everyone has one. The "big-name" Christians tell their stories from the pulpit, on television, and in magazine interviews. Oftentimes, they are dramatic and exciting—taking us from the depths of despair to amazing joy, even tears. They are thrilling, well-rehearsed, and for some, difficult to relate to. Don't misunderstand me. Without question,

Your wisdom has the potential to benefit countless others... if only you'll share it.

there is an important place for stories like these. They demonstrate the extremes to which God goes to make His story known.

But what about those of us who grew up attending church, who knew from "cradle roll" classes on that Jesus loves me and all the little children of the world? Our stories are often far less dramatic. Certainly, we were lost in our sin before we confessed Jesus as our Saviour. The joy of knowing we have Him as our Shepherd, Brother, and co-Heir thrills our souls. And yet, we don't know where to start when it comes to sharing our faith stories... or if what we have to say will really make a difference in someone else's life. In comparison to someone who found Jesus in prison and then completely turned his or her life around, our simple stories of life-long faith seem anti-climactic — not "all that special."

I don't know your story yet. (I do hope you will share it with me!) What I do know is that if you are a Christian, you have incredibly important stories to tell. Yes, *stories*. Plural. God's grace and power are not exclusive to a one-time salvation moment. Jesus is alive and active in your life every day! My desire with this book is to help you find your stories and tell them with confidence so that others benefit, and God is glorified.

Dramatic Stories Are Nice But...

Saul fought fiercely to defend his faith. Appalled by those who turned their backs on centuries of tradition and disregarded everything to which he had devoted his life, he was out for blood. As he saw it, Christ-followers were an abomination; these fallen-away Jews insulted the one true God with their new ways. Full of righteous indignation and fiery passion, he and his companions discussed the plan of attack they would launch on Christians in Damascus. They moved with purpose down the dusty path... no time for fast food breaks or photo stops. This wasn't a road trip; it was a mission to crush the Jesus movement before it went any further.

And then in a flash, *everything* changed for Saul.

"Now as he went on his way, he approached Damascus, and suddenly a light from Heaven shone around him. And falling to the ground he heard a voice saying to him, 'Saul, Saul, why are you perse-cuting me?' And he said, 'Who are you, Lord?' And he said, 'I am Jesus, whom you are persecuting.'" (Acts 9:3-6)

Zealous to the point of "breathing threats and murder" one second, and on his knees in the dirt the next, Saul couldn't mistake the voice or its authority. In that momentary glimpse into Heaven, Saul's heart completely changed. Just a peek at Jesus's glory blinded him, *literally*. It's no wonder then that Saul (later called Paul) wasted no time in sharing his story. Retelling it later to King Agrippa in Rome, Paul explained:

"I was not disobedient to the Heavenly vision, but declared first to those in Damascus, then in Jerusalem and throughout all the region of Judea, and also to the Gentiles, that they should repent and turn to God, performing deeds in keeping with their repentance." (Acts 26:19-20)

Paul's conversion turned everything he so passionately believed upside down in an instant. And *nothing* was the same for him *ever again*. He went from being a well-respected and feared Jewish leader, to a Christ-follower who dedicated the rest of his life to telling everyone he met of Jesus's grace and salvation. His powerful story demonstrates the immediate, drastic, and permanent change Jesus caused in Paul's life.

Like the person who discovered Jesus's love and experienced immediate freedom from drug addiction, Paul's story is easily remembered because of its uniqueness. Perhaps you've heard a modern-day Road-to-Damascus story and have been emotionally moved by the obvious display of God's love and His power to change lives. Perhaps that's your story. If so, I hope you bless others by telling it. Dramatic stories are great. They're exciting to hear and to share. But the reality is, those stories aren't the norm.

Your Story Is Important to Share

If you feel you have to have a story like Paul's to share your faith effectively, you might never speak up. And that would be a loss for the people in your life — and for you.

Your story is important to tell for *your* sake.

Just like the teacher who learns more than his or her students by preparing a lesson, your faith is re-energized each time you share your stories. You remember how God sought you out — personally and specifically. You remember when He answered prayer. You recall that He led you to the right place, at the right time, where you met the person who offered you truth, help, hope, or understanding. Thinking through, preparing, and then verbalizing your stories heightens your awareness of God's activity.

In Philemon 1:4-5, Paul comments that he is encouraged by the stories he's heard about

Dramatic stories are great. But the reality is, those stories aren't the norm.

Philemon's love and faith in Jesus. But take a look at what he says in verse six about the potential outcome of sharing one's faith:

> "And I pray that the sharing of your faith may become effective for the full knowledge of every good thing that is in us for the sake of Christ."

We often hear evangelism discussed and encouraged as a way to bless others with the Good News. And that's certainly an important reason to speak up (one we'll discuss in a bit). But you, as the sharer, also receive a blessing. The more you watch for and recognize God's presence, the more you see Him working not only in your life, but in others' lives as well. As Proverbs 11:25 says, "the one who waters will himself be watered."

Aside from allowing us the blessing of seeing God at work, our stories can serve as powerful reminders. Moses admonished the Israelites

8

repeatedly to remember the Lord and what He had done to free them from slavery in Egypt (e.g.: Exodus 13:3; Deuteronomy 5:15; 7:18; 8:18). Moses retold the story and encouraged the Israelites to keep repeating it so they would remember that the God of the universe was on their side. He knew that if they didn't retell their stories, they would forget God's power and rely on their own strength.

In *Experiencing God*, Richard Blackaby explains that going all the way back to the story of the cross helps him remember God's intense and unyielding love. He writes:

"I always view my circumstances against the backdrop of the cross, where God clearly demonstrated once and for all His deep love for me. I may not always understand my current situation or how things will eventually turn out, but I can trust in the love Christ proved to me when He laid down His life for me on the cross. In the death and resurrection of Jesus Christ, God forever convinced me that He loves me."

We need to revisit our stories for the same reason. When life is challenging, it's easy to focus on our temporary circumstances and forget the grace and hope God has extended to us.

Your story is important because it is part of a greater story.

My friend Chad Nall is a youth and family minister in Little Rock, Arkansas. One of the truths he wants his students to understand is why their story matters: "Our story is part of His story, so no story is too small or insignificant. You are part of something epic!"

Epic—as in "heroic or grand in scale or character"—aptly describes God's story. From creation to the present day, God has used people to fulfill His mission. You have a role to play. Speaking up, telling others about something God has taught you or helped you through may well be your starring role in His story. And as John Eldredge writes in his book *Epic*, "It is a dangerous thing to underestimate your role in the Story. You will lose heart, and you will miss your cues." When you downplay, or worse, dismiss God's activity in your heart and life as *coincidence*, *luck*, or *good upbringing*, you are missing your cue!

Your story could help someone see God.

Throughout history, stories have been passed down from one generation to the next. It's human nature to want to share something exciting or touching. Think about all the stories that circulate on social media. We *like* and *share* freely when it comes to cute kittens and laughing babies because they make us smile. How much more important, then, is it to share how God is working in your life?

Let me offer a brief example of how a personal story passed from one person to another can remind people of, or even reveal, God's love. I have a friend who experienced two consecutive miscarriages a number of years ago. Even though she later gave birth to a healthy child, incredible surges of grief rose again and again through the years. One day as we talked, the memories of those losses hit her. I wanted to comfort her, but I have no experience with that kind of heartbreak. I couldn't tell her I knew how she felt. What I could offer were some words another friend had shared about her own miscarriage and how the knowledge that her baby was in Heaven offered great solace. My hurting friend had never before considered that truth. The realization that she would meet those sweet souls in Heaven soothed her spirit and reminded her how deeply God cared for her — and her unborn children. Had my other friend not shared her story with me earlier, I would have been at a loss for words.

Making God Real & Relevant

Real-life, present-day faith stories allow seekers to understand that Jesus cares for people personally and in practical ways. Those who are searching—even if they don't know for what exactly—may well be intrigued to learn more about your God when they hear how He makes a real difference in your everyday life.

Additionally, our stories can inspire and rejuvenate other Christians. Paul writes in 1 Thessalonians 5:11 that we should encourage one another and build each other up in our faith. In Philippians 4:8 he offers a practical way to do that:

"Finally, brothers, whatever is true, whatever is honorable, whatever is just, whatever is pure, whatever is lovely, whatever is commendable, if there is any excellence, if there is anything worthy of praise, think about these things."

Simple words can have a profound impact. And the truth is, it's far more common for God to use real people and everyday situations to accomplish His purposes and draw people to Himself. The fact that God uses our ordinary lives to make Himself known is what makes our stories relevant.

Get Personal

What commendable thing is God doing in your life?

What praiseworthy things do you need to tell others about?

Who could you encourage with a personal story of God's grace or help in time of need?

Three Kinds of Stories

In October 2012, my husband, Brian, and I heard God telling us to take our lives in a new direction. No, He didn't speak through thunder or a flash of light. Instead, it was through words spoken by a young couple who were preparing to go to Africa as missionaries. They spoke about their average Christian upbringing and how God had nudged them together and then matched them with a church-planting team bound for Africa. As they talked, two separate things happened simultaneously to me that changed both the way I think about testimonials and where we live.

First, my friend Laura Kurk leaned over and whispered, "That sounds like something your husband would like to do." I know it was Laura speaking, but I truly believe the Holy Spirit used her willing voice to make me aware of what was going on in Brian's heart at that moment.

Second, as I listened to the couple (whose names I can't even remember), the young man made a comment that hit home with me. He noted that the team leader had a very powerful, and, yes, dramatic testimonial. From abandonment, violence, prison, and finally to redemption, his story had it all. "In comparison, my story doesn't seem all that exciting. But I've learned that my story is just as important to tell," he said.

The truth is, if he hadn't been willing to share his faith story—one that traced how he grew up knowing a Father who loved him, the Son who saved him, and a message of love he felt compelled to share—our lives might have hummed along at status quo. Instead, he courageously stood at the front of our Family Builders class and addressed a crowd of about 100 people, most of whom were at least a decade older than himself. He spoke humbly and from the heart. He acknowledged that as excited as he and his young wife felt about their upcoming adventure, they still had a lot to learn and a few fears to face.

His story resonated in our hearts—not because it was dramatic, in fact, low-key describes it more aptly. Still, his words inspired transformation in our lives. As he spoke, God worked on my husband's heart, calling us to work and live for Him in Ireland.

In *Reimagining Evangelism*, Rick Richardson discusses two main categories of Christian testimonies, or stories about how God has worked or is working in a person's life. Your *conversion story* explains how you came to know God and the truth of the Gospel. For some, this happened in a blinding flash — an *aha!* moment in which following Jesus made total sense. For others, the process required months or even years. And for some people, the exact moment of conversion or commitment to Christ is a little hazy. Trust in Jesus began at an early age and grew over time.

Then there are *transformation stories*. Every Christian has at least one, but it's more likely you have many. They are the moments when God has challenged, strengthened, comforted, provided for, and transformed you from the inside out. As the missionary-in-training spoke to our class that Sunday morning, his transformation story is what hit home with me. He shared how God had challenged him in subtle ways to consider moving to Africa to share the love and truth of the Gospel. His story wasn't mystical or dramatic, but even as he shared his faith that God would see them through

> *Your story is not really about you; it's about God.*

the preparation phase and the upcoming move to a place unlike any in which they'd ever lived, our own lives began to change. It felt as though God gently shook me awake and said, "Get ready. I have a job for you."

In addition to moments of conversion and transformation, I believe there are many times in our lives when God shows up simply to remind us that He loves us and that He is more awesome than we can fathom. I call those *affirmation stories*. Sometimes those moments are as simple and as breathtaking as an impossibly beautiful sunset. Or it could be the moment that God whispers to your soul and allows you to understand that the overwhelming love you feel for your child is nothing compared to how much He loves you. As the master artist, God is infinitely creative in the ways He chooses to affirm His presence.

Before we take a closer look at the definition and purpose of conversion, transformation, and affirmation stories, I want to impress upon you one important truth: Your story is not really about you; it's about God. We are created in God's image so that we might reflect and glorify Him, not ourselves. Your story is simply a way for people to see God more clearly.

As David Swanson, a facilitator for the Perspectives on World Missions course we attended in 2013, explained, we are like a straw in a milkshake. Imagine sipping a decadent milkshake. Chocolate, strawberry, passion fruit... you pick your favorite flavor. The creamy, delicious concoction slides through the straw and into your mouth. You feel refreshed and satisfied. When the cup is empty, you think, *that milkshake was amazing!* You don't say, "What a great straw!" In fact, unless the straw was too small or broken and difficult to drink through, you are unlikely to even notice the straw.

We are like the straw. The purpose of a faith story isn't to draw attention to oneself, but to be a conduit that moves the sweetness of God into people's lives.

Conversion Stories

"For God so loved the world, that he gave his only Son, that whoever believes in him should not perish but have eternal life." (John 3:16)

Do you remember the moment that Jesus's promise in John 3:16 became real to you? Do you remember the relief and peace that rushed in when you finally understood you could never be "good enough," but it was all right because Jesus stood in your place, took the blame for your guilt, and paid the ultimate price to grant you access to Heaven—and His presence in your life *now*?

Conversion stories culminate with the moment of realization: Jesus died for me to erase my sins. Salvation is a gift that He wants to give me. My new life can begin the moment I confess Him as my Saviour.

These stories are a joy to hear because they allow us a glimpse at how God works to open people's hearts to Him. As you'll read in the following examples, conversion stories often sound a lot like the song "Amazing Grace." The common thread that ties all of our stories together is despair replaced by joy. Listen closely and you'll hear the following unsatisfactory states of being expressed before Jesus came into the person's life:

- Hopelessness
- Depression
- Despondency
- Emptiness
- Fear
- A feeling that something important is missing
- A longing for something more

Paul explains the reason behind these feelings:

"And you were dead in the trespasses and sins in which you once walked, following the course of this world, following the prince of the power of the air, the spirit that is now at work in the sons of disobedience among whom we all once lived in the passions of our flesh, carrying out the desires of the body and the mind, and were by nature children of wrath, like the rest of mankind." (Ephesians 2:1-3)

Without God's love and Jesus's salvation, we aren't simply lost, we are spiritually *dead*. Zombies (the *Scooby-Doo* version, anyway) fascinate my 10-year-old son. Unseeing, they wander in search of self-satisfaction. That's not far off the mark when we consider life without Jesus. Unlike zombies, most non-Christians have no desire to hurt or take advantage of anyone. In fact, for many of us, our main quest before coming to know Jesus as Lord is a search for peace or a life of purpose and meaning. But when our hearts are unseeing — or spiritually dead — we blindly follow the course of this world. Ultimately, we discover that searching for satisfaction outside of God and the Word is futile.

Praise God that death and despair aren't the end of the story. No, what lies ahead for everyone who accepts it, is the gift of abundant and everlasting life in Jesus Christ.

> "But God, being rich in mercy, because of the great love with which he loved us, even when we were dead in our trespasses, made us alive together with Christ—by grace you have been saved..." (Ephesians 2:4-5)

The message of the conversion story is simple: "I once was lost, but now I'm found." This same message of victory over spiritual death through Jesus's death on the cross and His resurrection is heard in each and every conversion story — regardless of the words chosen to tell the tale. See if you can find that message in the following stories. I hope they'll encourage you and inspire you to think about how God introduced Himself to you.

'I Knew I Could Never Be Good Enough'

"I just knew it was right," says Phil (short for Philomena). "The moment I heard the message of the Gospel, I knew it was true. It made total sense." Phil grew up in a religious environment, but it was one that relied on her own works and goodness. As a child she was told that every time she sinned a black spot soiled her soul. By the time she was a teenager, she felt as if she had no hope at all for salvation. "I knew I could never be good enough to erase that blackness," she says. Completely disheartened by a religious system, she had all but

The message of the conversion story is simple: "I once was lost, but now I'm found."

written off any chance of ever being at peace with God or herself. When she headed off to college, she determined to have nothing to do with religion or God. Why bother when she had no hope?

But God had a better plan. The dormmate assigned to Phil was a Christian who invited her to attend a small group Bible study. During the following weeks, Phil heard the Good News:

Jesus died for your sins.

He took your place.

Salvation is a gift.

You don't have to work your way to Heaven — in fact, you can't!

She even, for reasons she couldn't explain, went out and bought herself a Bible — something she'd never owned or read on her own before. Each truth from the Word lightened and finally removed the depressing weight with which religion had burdened her heart. Accepting the gift of salvation

23

made sense. And more importantly, for the first time, she felt free and completely loved by God.

A "Chance" Meeting

Michael headed to the skate park for one last ride. Weighed down by the guilt of past mistakes, he wasn't sure he could go on.

Only a few weeks before, Michael found out his girlfriend was pregnant. Rather than risk being humiliated and ostracized by their families and friends, the young couple decided to terminate the pregnancy using an abortion pill. The abortion didn't go as planned, but ended even more tragically two months later when the tiny fetus was born in a bathroom and then disposed of.

Distraught, Michael left town to clear his head. Instead of feeling better, his mounting guilt became too much to bear. Ready to end it all, he planned to skateboard for a few hours and then... lights out.

Again, God had a better plan. Kobe, a skateboard missionary (Did you know there was even such a thing?), felt God pushing him to go to the skate park. It had already been a long day. Sleep sounded way better than skating at the moment. Tired as he was, he couldn't shake the feeling that he needed to go to the skate park. Finally he grabbed his board and thought, "Just for one hour."

Michael and Kobe were the only two skaters at the park that evening and after a few tricks and falls, Kobe invited Michael to grab a bite to eat. In broken Spanish the young men talked while they ate empanadas. Kobe told Michael about the skate park he and his team had built for the community and a little about why they were in the area. A couple hours later, they parted ways but not before agreeing to hang out again.

A few days later, Kobe's mission team moved to another city. He kept in touch with Michael who met up with the group in the new city each weekend for the next three weeks. Michael spent time with the group skating, sharing meals, and sitting in on their daily devotionals. By the third weekend, Michael had surrendered his heart to Jesus. He stood before the group at the final devotional and told them how God stopped him from committing suicide by bringing Kobe, the group, and ultimately the Saviour into his life.

'I knew I Was Going to Hell'

Gino lived the wild life as a teenager – drinking, smoking marijuana, and completely disrespecting all authority. But he assumed that as long as he didn't kill anyone he could probably get into Heaven. He settled down when he got married and returned to his Catholic upbringing.

A few years later, Gino suffered with depression to the point that he considered suicide. Not willing to put his wife and family through that trauma, he says, "One night in my room, with tears rolling down my face, I cried out to Jesus to help me. From that night on, I could feel a change in my life."

Time passed and Gino and his wife, Pauline, built a new home. "I remember stopping one day to look at our new house, the garden, and the mountains. It all looked so pretty. But inside, I was so unhappy," he says. Despite his beautiful surroundings, Gino felt far away from the One who had made it all. Heavy in his heart, he says, "I knew I was going to Hell. Then and there, I asked Jesus to show me the way to get to Heaven. If I couldn't be happy in this life, maybe I could be happy in the next."

A few days later, his sister invited him to a Bible study in her home. He went and was amazed by what he heard. "I came home to Pauline that night so full of joy, got down on my knees and asked Jesus into my life as my Lord and Saviour. From that night on my life has never been the same. The emptiness I had is gone. The piece that was missing from my heart was filled with Jesus. The depression went away," he says. "Pauline saw the changes that Jesus made in my life and so she asked Him to be her Saviour as well. Together we are growing in our new relationship with Christ."

A New Identity

Friendly and outgoing, Genesis said 'hi' and chatted easily with her fellow students in art school. So it bugged her that one young man wouldn't speak to her or anyone else. "He always seemed so aloof and I wanted to crack his shell and get him to say hello," she says. Day after day, she'd greet him with a smile and try to engage him in conversation. He ignored her efforts for the entire first semester of her freshman year.

When classes resumed after the winter break, something was different. She walked into the classroom and the boy greeted her with a friendly "Hi!" Rather than being pleased, she was shocked. "My response was something like, 'What's gotten into you?'" she remembers. "He said, 'Well, let me tell ya...,' and he started talking about how he'd become a Christian." As he spoke, Genesis wanted to know more. He was the same guy, and yet obviously different. "I invited myself to church with him the next Sunday to see what it was all about." There, she met a few girls from her school who asked if she wanted to study the Bible with them. As they read the Bible together, Genesis says, "I started to understand how Jesus takes an interest in us individually; that he died for me, personally."

Growing up, Genesis went to church occasionally with her grandmother, but really had no

Conversion stories reaffirm that God still actively works to draw people to Himself.

foundation of faith. In high school, "art girl" had been her identity, but at her college, everyone had the same role: art student. The first semester of college, she struggled with creating a persona. It wasn't that she wanted to stand out, exactly; she simply wanted to know who she was apart from everyone else. Unfortunately, the party-girl persona she'd invented wasn't someone she liked. "When I realized I could repent (or turn from) that way of life and I could be close to God—I felt completely relieved," she says. "I had a second chance. I didn't have to be the person I was, and I didn't have to be embarrassed or ashamed of my past. I felt clean."

Transformation Stories

I absolutely love hearing people's conversion stories. Each one reaffirms that God still actively works to draw people to Himself. But there's another type of story that all Christ-followers need to learn to tell. The moments when God reaches into our lives and reminds us of His power and His presence are what Rick Richardson refers to in *Reimagining Evangelism* as transformation stories. And as he explains, "Learning to recount experiences of God's reality and impact is what will help us and others most."

I grew up going to church. By the age of two, I could sing:

Wonderful, wonderful, Jesus is to me.
Counselor, Prince of Peace, Mighty God is He.
Saving me, keeping me from my sin and shame,
Wonderful is my redeemer, praise His name!

Granted, I didn't understand the complete meaning of the song until years later, but I never doubted that Jesus loved me. I knew early on that I wanted to belong to Him. So at nine years old, I confessed Jesus as God's Son and my Saviour and was baptized by our church's youth minister. As lackluster as that story is, I'm thankful it's mine. I'm also thankful it's not the only story I have to tell. I know that people who grew up without any faith, or who come from non-Christian backgrounds really can't relate to the innocence of a nine-year-old child's faith.

What people can identify with are common, human struggles. They can relate when I tell them how God helped me find Him again after I turned my back on Him as a teenager. They see His presence and care when I share how He pulled me out of the depression brought on by my divorce. And many people can relate when I share how my health and relationships were affected by what I call an "addiction to busyness." And I pray that our faith adventures here in Ireland encourage our Christian and non-Christian friends alike as we seek to trust and serve Him in a new and more dependent way.

In fact, there are many points in my life where God has made His love and care for me obvious. Often, this happens when life looks bleak or when I am fully convinced that I can't go another step further in my own power. Those moments when I surrender myself completely to His will are when He transforms me. His strength is most evident when I am at my weakest (2 Corinthians 12:9-10).

Affirmation Stories

Thankfully, your life doesn't have to be in the crosshairs for God to demonstrate His power and presence. Sometimes God shows Himself simply to reaffirm our faith and encourage us to trust Him more fully. Those are our affirmation stories. Here's one of mine...

God Works for Our Good and His Glory

Before flying across the ocean, Brian wanted to make a trip to Nebraska to visit his family. When we left home, we couldn't have imagined the events that would unfold or how the road trip would strengthen our faith.

We hit a huge storm about eight hours into our 14-hour trip. For more than an hour, we watched lightning streak across the Kansas sky and scanned the black thunderheads for funnel clouds. Rain pelted the car and standing water on the road tugged roughly at our little car. With no towns for miles in any direction, we plodded forward at 15–20 miles per hour, wipers at full speed. I'm from Texas, and no stranger to a summer "gully washer," but this was truly frightening. Looking over my white knuckles, I gripped the steering wheel and silently begged, "Lord, please be with us and protect us."

Tension in the car continued to climb until Brian grabbed our son Jacob's hand and put his other hand on my shoulder. He prayed aloud, not just for protection, but to be reminded that God was (IS) greater than any storm. With the final, "Amen," the car, though still buffeted by the storm, felt peaceful inside.

Later, on the other side of the rain, we found a motel, and called it a night. Before turning in, we thanked God for His safekeeping and power.

After breakfast the next morning, we pulled out of the parking lot and noticed the glowing tire-pressure warning on the dash. Eager to get on the road, and suspecting that the cooler temperatures could have lowered the pressure just enough to trigger the light, we agreed to stop if it was still on by the time we got to the next town.

The red warning light continued to burn steadily, so when we reached the tiny Kansas town about fifty miles down the road, we found a gas station with an air pump. With a borrowed tire gauge, Brian checked each tire and found them all at 32 PSI; the tire wall recommended 44 PSI. One by one, he added air to the tires.

Just as Brian finished with the fourth tire, a man pulled up behind our car in a green pickup truck. The farmer called out to us, "I used to have those same tires."

We smiled politely and then turned our focus back to the tires. As Brian measured the air pressure, I watched and thought, *Who in the world notices other people's tires?*

Undeterred by our lack of interest, he said, "Don't fill them up to 44 PSI like it says on the tire."

We nodded and smiled again. I didn't really put much stock in this stranger's advice. I mean, they put the numbers on the tires for a reason, right? (Later, Brian told me that at this point his ears perked up. He thought, *I can barely read the PSI recommendation. This guy's twenty feet away. How in the world does he know what's printed on the sidewall?*)

"I had mine filled at 44 and had four blowouts all at once," he continued. "I know it says 44 PSI on the tire, but if you do that they'll blow at 60–70 miles per hour. My guy at the dealership recommended keeping them at 32."

At "four blowouts" my mind instantly pictured us in a mangled mass of metal in the middle of nowhere. He had our attention.

We exchanged a few words to confirm that we'd heard him right, then off he drove. He offered a slow, friendly wave when I shouted, "Thank you!"

Brian went back around the car and let air out of each tire until they were back to 32 PSI. When we started the car, the warning light was off.

Driving down the road, I replayed the scene in my head. How on earth could someone twenty feet away tell what kind of tires we had? How could he know the tire walls had 44 PSI as the recommended pressure? What are the odds that the stranger, in that tiny Kansas town, would pull into the same gas station at the same time we did? I didn't even see him at the fuel pumps.

And then a lesson from our Perspectives class came to mind: God works for our good and His

God wants us to know Him, to see Him, to remember that He is alive and active in our lives today.

glory. He wants us to know Him, to see Him, to remember that He is alive and active in our lives today. He wants us to give Him the glory (praise/honor) for what He does.

I don't know why the light came on, and frankly, thinking about that scares me a little (Ephesians 6:12). Without the man's warning, Brian would've filled all four tires to 44 PSI, and off we would have gone, driving 60–70 miles per hour like we had been all morning.

I know that at any moment, God could have flicked that warning light off. If it had turned off while we were driving, we would have credited it to cooler weather or a glitch in the sensor.

But He waited. And we pulled into a gas station where a man in a green pickup offered a little friendly advice. Perfectly orchestrated help delivered exactly when we needed it.

At that time, we were only a few weeks away from getting on the plane bound for Ireland. Even though we were excited about working with the church-planting team, we were nervous about what our lives would be like. And let me say that getting rid of most of our stuff, prepping for the move, and saying our goodbyes was more than a little stressful. Although we felt sure God led us to the decision to move, questions of how, why us, and what on earth were we thinking, intensified as our departure date neared. And then God stepped in with a little reminder: *I've got you in the palm of my hand. Stop stressing. Trust me.*

I do trust Him; more now than ever.

Do You Know Your Stories?

If you have been a Christian for more than a few years, you probably have several stories to share. Do you know what they are? Can you tell them well?

The next chapter offers questions and guidance for writing and sharing your stories. Please take the time to write down what you learn and recall. Doing so will help prepare you to tell your story when the time comes.

Get Personal

How long have you been a Christian?

When was the last time you shared a
faith story (conversion, transformation, or
affirmation) with someone?

How do you feel when you talk about what
God has done or is doing in your life with:
other Christians—

non-Christian friends and co-workers—

family members—

What's Your Story?

When Jesus walked the streets of Jerusalem and taught along the shores of the Sea of Galilee, He touched people's lives in real and practical ways. Crowds listened as He told stories to illustrate and address tough but common issues ranging from lust and adultery, to money and greed, to worry and fear. Beyond teaching people how to treat their neighbors and family members, He took care of their physical and spiritual needs. He does the same in our lives today. Our task is to recognize His hand at work, to pay attention when the Holy Spirit whispers to our souls, and then to share those personal stories with others.

Yes, I said it: *personal.* The world we live in is hard. From the time sin entered the world, it has been crouching at the door (Genesis 4:7). All too often we welcome it in with open arms. Then, like Peter, we come to ourselves and weep bitterly (Matthew 26:69-75). We learn from our mistakes and from what the Holy Spirit reveals to us in Scripture. Through God's grace, we find the Way out of temptation (1 Corinthians 10:13, John 14:6). We turn to God in prayer when we can't take another step, and He provides unfathomable peace (Philippians 4:7).

All of those moments transform the way we live and think. And they are exactly the kinds of things we don't share because, "it's too personal." And so, we talk about our children, or sports, or if you happen to be in Ireland, you talk about the always-safe topic: weather.

The outcome of all this small talk is *social connections* in churches, instead of *meaningful relationships* that can embolden us to love and live like Jesus. When we don't share our honest, sin-scarred stories, we present the illusion of perfection. And that hurts us (the church and the individuals that comprise it) in several ways:

- Keeping up appearances is stressful, exhausting work. Seriously, who has the time and energy to pretend to be faultless?

- The false belief that everyone else "has it all together," causes people to expect they'll be judged rather than loved by their church family. Instead of risking to expose their weaknesses, they "fake it" at church, knowing that when they get with their friends in the real world they can be themselves. How sad is that?

• When Christians are hurt by or are grappling with sin, they feel they have no one with whom to share their struggles. When everyone around them is (and always has been) "perfect," whom can they turn to that could possibly understand their mess?

Outside the church, talking about T-ball, or whether or not it's going to rain this weekend is fine, but when we stop there we miss out on opportunities to make an eternal difference in people's lives. Now, please hear me: I'm not saying you

"God is always doing 10,000 things in your life, and you may be aware of three of them."

~John Piper

should accost every person you encounter with your God stories the moment you meet them. We are meant to be the *aroma* of Christ both inside and outside the church—not a stench that puts people off (2 Corinthians 2:15). However, I do believe that when we share our struggles and how God has comforted and pulled us through hard times, our relationships can be stronger and our Christianity more effective.

My challenge to you—and myself—is to get personal. Share the hard stuff, the stories that hurt to tell, as well as those that are joy-filled. God isn't superficial; we shouldn't be either.

Questions to Spark Your Memory & Awareness

You already have a story.

That's good news because it means you don't have to make it up, fake it, or try to tell it in a way that impresses people. The next few pages are devoted to helping you think about your stories. Start by looking back to see how God has been at work in your life. Answer the questions honestly. Allow yourself to feel the emotions of the memories. Write down everything you can recall. This is your time for thinking on paper. You may not end up using everything you write now; that's okay. The point of this exercise is to help you remember at least some of the ways that knowing Jesus has made a difference in your life.

Because God loves each individual so much, he helps us find Him. As Paul explains:

"And he made from one man every nation of mankind to live on all the face of the earth, having determined allotted periods and the boundaries of their dwelling place, that they should seek God, and perhaps feel their way toward him and find him. Yet he is actually not far from each one of us...." (Acts 17:26-27)

God orchestrates our lives in such a way that we have opportunity to reach out and find Him. Where you lived, what you were doing, and how you felt before you met God or knew Jesus's love are all important components of your story.

What was your early life like?

What did you know about Jesus as a child?

What/who were your spiritual influences?

How did those early influences affect the way you thought about God and about yourself?

When did you become a Christian? What did that mean to you?

How did your life change when you became a Christian?

If you grew up in a Christian household and feel like you've "always been a Christian," when did the truth of the Gospel first feel real and personal to you?

Who first shared the Good News with you?

What was your response the first time you heard the Gospel?

Describe how you felt when it "clicked" that Jesus is "the way, the truth, and the life" and that in Him you could have freedom now and eternal life in Heaven.

Think beyond your conversion story. How has God make Himself real to you recently?

How has being a Christian made a difference in your life? What do you do/believe/feel now, that you didn't before?

When have you felt closest to God? Describe the circumstances and why you felt He was close to you.

When have you felt that God was distant? How did you feel during that time? How did God close the gap between you and Him?

Describe a time when you saw how God was working or had worked in your life for your ultimate good.

What is your relationship with Jesus now?

How has the Holy Spirit been a counselor or comforter to you?

When and how have you seen prayers answered, even if the answer wasn't what you expected?

Put It All Together

Acknowledging what God has done and is doing in your life is essential to your ability to share your story. Life passes so quickly. Often, it isn't until we look back that we see how He guided, protected, or comforted us. For me, the discovery exercise above is powerful because it reminds me that God cares about me personally and that I am never really alone. Before you continue, why not pause for a moment and thank God for what He has done in your life and for the magnitude of His love for you?

Now, it's time to write your faith story. If you answered all the questions above, you probably discovered several specific times when God made Himself obvious to you. For now, focus on just one of those times and let's turn it into a story you can share with confidence.

Every good story comprises three important aspects:

1. A beginning
2. A middle
3. An end

I was dead.
Jesus saved me.
Now I'm alive and free.

Obviously, your story needs a bit more to it to make it interesting, but not much. Your answers to the questions in the previous section probably yielded far more information than you need — or at least more than people would want to hear in one sitting. (Remember: aroma — not stench.) Your story isn't about holding people captive for hours. It's about sharing how God has shown up in real and relevant ways throughout your life.

Your story is unique, because you are one of a kind — and because God is brilliantly creative. He seeks people out in ways that work specifically for them. Our stories are diverse, so you won't find a formula or a specific pattern to follow here. However, I have included a few considerations for crafting an effective story — effective meaning people listen when you tell it, and it points to God. Let these storytelling principles assist you, not restrict or constrain you.

> *Your story is unique, because you are one of a kind — and because God is brilliantly creative.*

Start at the Beginning... But Not at Birth

Several of my editing clients have been skincare and cosmetic companies. Many of these companies use "before" and "after" pictures to show the results their customers see when using their products: e.g. fuller-looking eyelashes, reduced appearance of cellulite, or smoother skin. The bare-faced "before "picture shows all the skin's flaws. The "after" pictures offer proof of the advertised product's efficacy.

When someone asks why you follow Christ, what will you tell them? What will you say if some-one asks, "What real difference has Jesus made in your life?" Where will you start?

Let me encourage you not to share your entire life story. Instead, think in terms of those before and after pictures. What was the state of your life before you became a Christian? What does that "bare-faced" picture look like? You don't need to go into every detail of your sin, but don't gloss over it either.

When Did Jesus Come into the Picture?

Once you've set the scene, move to the middle. How were you introduced to Jesus? Or, if you want to share a transformation moment, when and how did God show Himself? Did you experience a "God-incidence"—a God-orchestrated coinci-dence? What was your initial reaction? What did you do with what you learned?

Describe the "After" Picture

Life changes with Jesus. Your story should relate how Jesus has made a difference in your life. If the fruits (or practical evidence) of the Spirit are love, joy, peace, patience, kindness, goodness, faithfulness, gentleness, and self-control, which of these is God cultivating in you—and how?

Resist the urge to paint an overly rosy picture. Life isn't a happily-after-ever fairytale. If you still struggle with the same sin you were dealing with before you met Jesus, it's okay to admit it. Share how He is helping you overcome that temptation. What do you do when old desires resurface?

Read It and Share It

Once you've written your story, read it aloud to hear how it sounds. Then, share it with a friend. Ask if anything seems confusing or unclear. Your goal isn't to memorize your stories so you can repeat them verbatim. The purpose of this exercise is to think about what's most important to share. For those of us who have trouble talking off-the-cuff, a little preparation can make it easier to express what's on our hearts.

A Few More Tips for Telling Your Faith Story:

Be Brief

Keep it short and focus on what really matters. How many times have your grandparents tried to tell you a story that took *ages* because they got bogged down with a detail like whose cousin's house they were at or what type of car they were driving? Unless the detail is relevant, don't stress over it. Be accurate, but don't stand there deliberating over a detail that doesn't matter... it's a sure way to lose your listener's attention.

Be Clear About the Point of Your Story

Any story with too many subplots or characters is hard to follow. You may have a dozen stories to tell about how the Holy Spirit has worked in your life. That's fantastic. But don't try to tell them all at once. Getting off on a rabbit trail dilutes the power of a story. Stay focused and stick to the main plot. As you continue your relationship with the listener, you'll have opportunities to tell other stories.

Be Real, Not Religious

Pious talk is always irritating, but it's especially important to drop any church lingo when you're speaking to seekers. Words that are commonly spoken from pulpits aren't necessarily familiar to people who've never been to church. Sanctification, righteousness, eschatology, carnality, iniquity, temperance, etc., are all words that can cause confusion. You know forbearance means patience, so keep it simple and say patience.

A Transformation Story from My Life

I worked hard to finish my college degree. Recently divorced, I was a single mom. I worked as a freelance photographer and graphic designer and enrolled in as many classes as I could cram in while the daycare was open. Looking back, I know that's when I developed an intense desire to be totally independent and in control of my life.

When I began my writing and editing career, things only got worse. Remarried now and with a second child, I worked crazy-long hours (some days from 9 a.m. to 3 a.m.). I loved feeling needed. Busyness made me feel worthy of respect.

I kept up the "crazy-busy" intensity for a few years, but my health, family relationships and quality of life suffered. My relationship with God never made it beyond the pew on Sunday morning. Finally, I went to the doctor because I could no longer ignore the heart palpitations, hair loss and the buzzing in my ears—all brought on by stress.

Rather than talking about lifestyle changes, she prescribed a pill to help me feel better. Warning signals shot through my mind.

I knew something had to change; a pill wasn't the answer. In the quiet of my backyard one summer day, I begged God to help me get over myself and my need to control... to help me rest in Him. I'd done it before but in all the busyness of life, I had forgotten how.

"Simplify" was the word that rang in my heart. I felt God saying, "Trust me to take care of you. Get to know Me again."

Without any other solutions, I gave in. I began reading my Bible daily for the first time in my life. I took notes and journaled about what I read and what God's Word meant for me personally.

Honestly, I still struggle with the lure of busyness. I feel guilty if I spend a Saturday reading or playing with my family. I know I'm His work in progress; He won't quit on me. (Philippians 1:6) God is faithful. He reminds me through His Word that my worth doesn't come from what I accomplish. It comes from Him. There's peace in knowing I don't have to do or be anything for Him to love me. That peace helps me say "no" to excess work and "yes" to trusting and resting Him.

Get Personal

Now it's your turn. Use this space to write one of your faith stories.

_____

_____

_____

_____

_____

_____

_____

_____

_____

_____

_____

_____

_____

_____

_____

_____

_____

_____

_____

_____

_____

_____

_____

_____

_____

_____

_____

_____

_____

_____

_____

_____

_____

_____

_____

_____

_____

_____

_____

_____

_____

_____

_____

_____

_____

_____

_____

_____

Finding the Courage to Share

a few months after arriving in Ireland, we attended a meeting where Steve Timmis, co-author of *Everyday Church* and *Total Church*, shared thoughts about life-on-life missions. As one of the leaders of Crowded House in England, he explained how ministry thrives when ordinary people share their day-to-day lives and focus on making God part of the everyday conversation.

The members of this Christian family strive to be involved in one another's lives in real and practical ways, not just while they're in "church mode." Their focus moves well beyond "friendship evangelism," the kind of simple and too-often silent outreach that never gets beyond being a kind and friendly person. Instead, Crowded House's priority is sharing the Gospel and speaking Jesus's name in the context of daily life both with Christians as well as people who aren't yet believers. This is how they explain their values on thecrowdedhouse.org:

"We are committed to filling ordinary life with gospel intentionality, pastoring one another with the gospel and sharing the gospel with unbelievers. We challenge one another to be sacrificial, servant-hearted, risk-taking and flexible because the gospel has priority over our comfort, preferences, security and traditions. We will not let Christian activity be just one part of our lives."

After his talk, Steve opened the floor for questions. Most people asked about logistics: What exactly do you do? When and where do you meet? Describe a typical worship service. How do you involve people? What, specifically, do you do to make people feel included?

Then a 20-something, short-term missionary spoke up and made me cringe at the brashness of a very honest question — one that I'd been wondering, but didn't dare verbalize. She asked, "Where do you get your confidence?" She, like the rest of us, wanted to know where he (and the others in his church family) found the courage to speak — seemingly fearlessly — about God and the Gospel in a post-Christian culture. Where did they get the nerve to speak up?

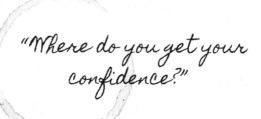

"Where do you get your confidence?"

If Steve was taken aback by the question, he didn't show it. He responded kindly and with the best, most encouraging answer possible: "I'm in Christ." He explained that they try all sorts of things and talk with all sorts of people. Sometimes their efforts spark positive conversations and sometimes the Gospel message is outright rejected. "But at the end of the day, my confidence comes from knowing that I'm in Christ," he said.

"If God is for us, who can be against us? He who did not spare his own Son but gave him up for us all, how will he not also with him graciously give us all things? Who shall bring any charge against God's elect? It is God who justifies. Who is to condemn? Christ Jesus is the one who died—more than that, who was raised—who is at the right hand of God, who indeed is interceding for us." (Romans 8:31-34)

If you aren't certain about what to say or are uncomfortable telling your faith stories, remember that if you are a Christ-follower, He is your fearless ally.

You Are in Christ

Just before ascending into Heaven, Jesus outlined a job for His followers:

> "**Go** therefore and **make disciples** of all nations, **baptizing** them in the name of the Father and of the Son and of the Holy Spirit, **teaching** them to observe all that I have commanded you. And behold, **I am with you always**, to the end of the age." (Matthew 28:16-20, emphasis added)

As Christ's followers, we are tasked with the same job to make disciples, baptize, and teach people about Him and His ways. It's impossible to fulfill this responsibility without speaking up. Sure,

If non-Christians follow our examples without knowing the reason behind our actions, they will remain lost in sin.

we can be a good, kind, Christian examples. But if non-Christians follow our examples of love and generosity without knowing the reason and joy behind our actions, they will remain lost in sin.

It can be scary to talk about Jesus in a world that thinks so little of Him. People's reactions range from apathetic to enraged at the idea that He is the *only* way to an eternal life with God. And then there's the concept of eternal life… how wacky does that sound to the person who believes that death is the end? The resurrection story adds all sorts of complications: No one can come back from the dead after three days, right? Surely that's a story made up by people.

Yes, speaking up will undoubtedly lead to difficult questions, disbelief, and maybe even derision. When those moments come, remember Jesus's promise: *"I am with you always."*

In His prayer in John 17, Jesus asked God to be with you and me (v. 20) "so that the world may believe that you have sent me." Scripture makes it clear that God desires for everyone to know about and accept the gift Jesus offers (1 Peter 2:9). And history has proven that He will go to impossible lengths to fulfill His purposes. When we join God in His mission of drawing people to Himself, why wouldn't He bless our efforts, however feeble, to accomplish it?

Strengthened by the Holy Spirit

Jesus knew that if left up to us and our uncertainties and insecurities, the Good News wouldn't make it out of Jerusalem. That's why He didn't leave it up to us alone. He told Peter:

"And when they bring you before the synagogues and the rulers and the authorities, do not be anxious about how you should defend yourself or what you should say, for the Holy Spirit will teach you in that very hour what you ought to say." (Luke 12:11-12)

I have to believe that the Holy Spirit will do the same for us when we seek to tell others about how knowing Jesus makes a difference in our lives. The Bible makes it clear that our confidence comes from God; it isn't something we have to muster up out of our own will and power.

It's helpful to remember your role isn't to save people. Only Jesus can do that.

So, where do you get your confidence to speak up about Jesus? From Him! Ask Jesus to embolden you through the power of the Holy Spirit to notice and take advantage of opportune moments to share how God has worked or is working in your life. When we prayerfully seek the Holy Spirit's guidance with a heart that is willing to follow His lead, we put ourselves in a position to be used for God's glory. Ask the Holy Spirit to give you the right words and the courage to speak them.

Knowing Your Part

As a Christian, you have a specific task: let your light shine, be salty, proclaim the Good News.

Bill Hybels writes in *Just Walk Across the Room*, "I believe that the highest value in personal evangelism is to be attuned to the movement and prompting of the Holy Spirit and to play only the role you are intended to play in another person's life."

It's helpful to remember your role isn't to save people. Only Jesus can do that. You aren't the message. You are just the straw for the milkshake, remember? Your part is simply to speak up—to say Jesus's name, to share how He's working in your life today.

It's comforting to know that God is the one who draws people to Himself. We are only the messengers—and we have the best possible news to share!

Get Personal

Think of a time when you shared a personal faith story and were kidded or even belittled for your beliefs.

How did/does that experience affect your willingness to speak up?

Read Acts 4. Because of the extraordinary opposition the apostles and believers faced, they prayed for boldness. They began in verse 24 by praising God and reminding themselves of His power. Take some time now to remember how God has shown you His power, love, and mercy. Ask Him for the courage to share with others what He has done.

Sharing Your Story

Not long ago, a couple, Ben and Rebecca, and I were discussing the power of stories. They told me that the church they'd attended in Arizona set aside time each month in their worship service during which people shared how God made a difference in their lives.

On those Sundays, the church leadership ensured that additional people were available to pray with those who were touched by what they heard. As people learned how God had helped someone through a health scare, or brought others out of a life of sinful self-gratification, or replaced depression with joy, or emboldened someone to share the Gospel, or made someone finally realize that life without Him was futile and life *with* Him is eternal and free, hearts opened. "People understood that if God could work in other people's lives, He could help them too," Rebecca explained.

For many, those Sundays were the beginning of a new way of life. Ben then pointed out, that's exactly why we need to share our faith stories. "We limit the Holy Spirit's power when we keep His activity to ourselves," he said. If we, like Abraham, are blessed so that we might be a blessing to others, shouldn't we begin by giving people the chance to understand how knowing Jesus makes a difference in our lives?

Tell Your Friends

After Jesus freed the demon-possessed man in Mark 5 (also in Luke 8), he told him not to keep the miracle to himself.

"As he [Jesus] was getting into the boat, the man who had been possessed with demons begged him that he might be with him. And he did not permit him but said to him, 'Go home to your friends and tell them how much the Lord has done for you, and how he has had mercy on you.' And he went away and began to proclaim in the Decapolis how much Jesus had done for him, and everyone marveled." (Mark 5:18-20)

"We limit the Holy Spirit's power when we keep His activity to ourselves."

The man's life had been so undeniably changed by the Lord, people couldn't help but notice and ask about the difference they saw in him. And I'm sure, he never forgot his before-and-after story. How could he possibly keep it to himself?

Always Be Prepared

"...In your hearts honor Christ the Lord as holy, always being prepared to make a defense to anyone who asks you for a reason for the hope that is in you; yet do it with gentleness and respect..." (1 Peter 3:15)

Knowing our stories and learning how to confidently share them is one way to prepare for questions about the reason for our hope—the difference people see in our lives. When we follow Jesus, not only with our hearts but with our actions and words as well, people will notice. The Light within makes us appear different somehow from the rest of the world. Sooner or later, as the Apostle Peter suggests, others will see evidence of our assured hope of salvation. Maybe they'll notice how peaceful you seem even in the most stressful situations. Perhaps they'll see the joy you feel even in the midst of loss when a Christian friend or loved one passes from this world on to Heaven. Maybe they'll notice your commitment to integrity at work, or simply the fact that you take time to stop and listen to people when they speak. And hopefully, they'll hear you mention the name of Jesus and wonder what the connection is between Him and your glow. Sharing your stories allows people to better understand that connection.

What Keeps Us from Sharing?

Early on, I mentioned that your story is not really about you. The purpose of sharing any faith story is to point to God and His love and power. The hope is that someone will hear about your experience and realize that they, too, could have a personal relationship with the Creator of the universe. Or at the very least, that they will understand that God isn't distant and uninterested but loving and deeply concerned for every individual. For me, the knowledge and the truth that I am the messenger,

> *The purpose of sharing any faith story is to point to God and His love and power.*

not the message, relieves much of my self-induced stress. Still, fears and doubts creep up from time to time. See if you can relate to any of the following common but poor excuses I've used for not speaking up.

I Don't Want to Seem Too Religious

Do you hesitate to share your story because you're afraid of what others will think? I know I've been guilty of that. I don't want people to think I'm too religious or, heaven forbid, *radical*.

When I worked in direct sales, I often heard from consultants on my team who were struggling in their businesses. The problem wasn't their belief in the product; they loved it! The problem was that they didn't want to seem "pushy." So they kept their mouths shut and hoped customers would show up and ask to buy from them. These consultants soon discovered "hope marketing" doesn't work.

I realize, however, that I've practiced the same kind of hope-and-wait strategy in my faith. But God's Word has a way of convicting me of behaviors and attitudes that He wants to change in me. John 12:42-43 pricked my heart one day and convinced me that what other people think really shouldn't matter:

"Nevertheless, many even of the authorities believed in him, but for fear of the Pharisees they did not confess it, so that they would not be put out of the synagogue; for they loved the glory that comes from man more than the glory that comes from God." (John 12: 42-43)

I do not want to be one of the people who cares more about the glory that comes from man! We are tasked with making disciples. Hoping people will see Jesus in us without actually ever talking about Him isn't going to accomplish that.

To be salt and light, we must share what God has done.

In *Crazy Love,* Francis Chan shares a revelation he had while visiting India: "The majority of believers on this earth find it laughable that we could reduce the call to follow Jesus and make disciples to an invitation to sit in church service." He explains:

"I visited thousands of Christians who had been beaten or watched relatives murdered for their faith. At one point, I said to one of the leaders, 'Every believer seems so serious about his or her commitment to Christ. Aren't there people who just profess Christ but don't really follow Him?' He answered by explaining that nominal Christianity doesn't make sense in India. Calling yourself a Christian means you lose everything. Your family and friends reject you, and you lose your home, status, and job. So why would anyone choose that unless he or she is serious about Jesus?"

Chances are your circumstances are far less challenging than those living in India, China, North Korea, Syria, Nigeria, or any of the other countries where Christians are martyred today. I know mine are. The worst it gets for most of us in the Western world is that someone disagrees with us or calls us foolish for believing what the Bible teaches. Isn't that a small price to pay for the chance to introduce someone to the freedom and hope Jesus offers?

Isn't Faith Personal?

I'm a peacemaker, an encourager, a teacher; those are my spiritual gifts. Evangelism? Not so much. But nowhere in the Bible are those who don't possess the gift of evangelism or preaching exempted from Jesus's command in Matthew 28:16-20. Bummer.

Instead, He says you are salt and light (Matthew 5: 13-16). "You are." Not, "I'd like for you to be," or "It would be great if you could be salty every once in a while." If we're going to be salt and light, we've got to get over this "faith is personal" nonsense.

Does that mean I have to start preaching on the street? No. (Thank goodness!) But it does mean that I should use my gifts to help people find the peace that Jesus offers. It also means I can encourage people by being real with them—sharing my struggles and allowing them to see how God helps me deal with life. I can also encourage people by paying attention, noticing their needs, and responding to them with practical help and spiritual hope.

In *God Pocket*, Bruce Wilkinson invites people to partner with God in His mission to make Himself known to others. His challenge is to always carry with you a bit of money you've committed to God's use. Then wait and be willing to respond when the Holy Spirit nudges you to deliver that money to someone in need. As you hand over the money,

Faith is personal—it's shared from one person to another.

give God the credit by saying something like, "This money belongs to God, and I think He wants me to give it to you. God wants you to know He really loves you."

Responding to someone's financial needs is one way to show people that yes, faith *is* personal—it's shared from one person to another. In fact, any need you recognize and respond to while giving God the credit for making you aware of the person allows them to see Him at work in *their* lives. Who knows? In reaching out, you may become part of the faith story they share one day.

What If My Story Leads to Questions I Can't Answer?

When God becomes part of our everyday conversation, it's only natural that people will ask to know more about Him. That's exciting, but it can also be scary. What if someone asks a Bible question to which you don't know the answer? What if you start a faith conversation with your story and the person asks a hard question in return? One that sounds something like: "I prayed for God to heal my mother/father/sister/brother/friend and He didn't. Why did God answer your prayers but not mine?" Responding with "God's ways are not our ways," won't win you any friends in those moments. But it is okay to be honest and say, "I don't know." It's even better to pray for clarity and to ask God to comfort and guide that person to the peace and understanding they seek.

If you don't know the answer to a question, admit it. Offer to study more and follow up, or to read the Bible with them to look for answers. Your honesty and willingness to help them in their search for understanding will make you even more approachable and allow people to open up to you — and to God.

Really, when I put my excuses for not speaking up to the test, none prove valid. To be salt and light, we must share what God has done.

Connect First

In his book *Breakthrough Communication*, Harrison Monarth writes, "Instead of communicating from our own perspective, we should always meet others where they are and take their beliefs, values, and experiences into consideration. It's the only

Honesty will make you approachable and allow people to open up to you —and to God.

way to eventual agreement; it's an immutable truth for getting anywhere in the world of work and business." In truth, taking others' perspectives, beliefs, backgrounds, and experiences into consideration can help you communicate more effectively, regardless of the topic.

Up to this point, the focus of this book has been on you telling your story. But any time you speak, whether it's in the business world or in your personal life, it's essential to be aware of your listener. Notice their body language: Are their arms crossed over their chest, closing them off from conversation? Or, are they leaning forward and making eye contact? If someone has "zoned out" or is obviously uninterested in the discussion, change the topic. Better yet, ask them a question about themselves. Droning on when someone has tuned out drives home the point that you care more about yourself than the other person.

To engage people's hearts and minds, you must first connect with them. Here are a few more tips for effective communication.

Listen When Others Talk

Have you ever seen someone "check out" while you were speaking to them? They scan their email inbox, or scroll through their Facebook newsfeed, or their eyes glaze over and you can tell they're no longer mentally with you. (Please tell me I'm not the only one this happens to!)

Don't be that person. You can't expect someone to listen to your stories if you zone out when they're talking.

When people (family members, friends, co-workers, complete strangers, *anybody*) talk, show them you care by listening attentively and completely. Ask questions about them, their experiences, and what they believe. Listen to their responses and resist the urge to formulate your rebuttal while they're speaking. If you're thinking about what you want to say, you aren't *really* listening.

Don't Expect People to Believe or Agree with You

This is hard for me. I believe what I believe because I think it's right and true. So it bothers me when people disagree or don't see things my way—especially if it's something I'm passionate about. But if I turn that line of thinking around, it stands to reason that when I challenge someone's beliefs they won't necessarily like it.

If we approach life from a Christian worldview, we can't expect people to readily agree with us. Neither can we condemn seekers for living worldly lives. (1 Corinthians 5:12) How else would they live?! The world is their reference point.

Practice being considerate of a person's worldview without wavering on your own. In other words, don't say, "That's stupid!" when they offer an opinion contrary to what the Bible teaches. (That may sound obvious, but the lack of tact some people exhibit when their ideas are challenged can be shocking.)

Instead of judging people or belittling their perspective, share the joy you've found in Christ. Ask if you may share another viewpoint or something you've learned or experienced. Show them the

Your role isn't to convict or convince people, but to shine the spotlight on Jesus.

scriptures that helped you find your joy, peace, and purpose. Remember, it isn't your role to convict or convince people, but to shine the spotlight on Jesus. And if they aren't interested in budging in their line of thought, be okay with agreeing to disagree.

Live Authentically

Finally, earn the right to share your faith stories by developing authentic relationships with others. I'm not saying you should "hide your light" until people get to know you. Do that and they'll rightly accuse you of presenting yourself under false pretenses. No, let's work on making our Christianity central to everything we do, say, and are. Rather than compartmentalizing our lives so neatly into boxes labeled work, family, friends, spiritual concerns, let's mix it up. Allow Jesus to be part of every relationship and aspect of your life.

Brian and I were "set up" by friends we shared in common. I knew Amy through Cub Scouts. Brian worked with Alan. Of all the people in their lives, we were the only two single Christians they knew. In their minds, it made sense that we should be together. I don't remember inviting Amy to worship service. I don't think Brian ever specifically offered to study the Bible with Alan. But they knew through our conversations and behavior that we were Christ-followers. (I don't say that to brag because like I mentioned in the introduction, I look back on the conversations we had and think, "I wish I'd said...." I'm just thankful Jesus was evident in our lives in some small way.)

Because we opened our separate lives to this couple, God was able to use them to help Brian and me find one another. God brought them into our lives at just the right time and started a new faith story... one that we're still working with God to write.

It's challenging, but I believe that the most effective way to connect in this superficial world is to make our lives and stories real. Complete authenticity discredits the stereotype of hypocritical Christians and allows people to see us for what we are: fallible people blessed to know the infallible God because of His great love and immense grace.

Get Personal

What are some of the reasons or excuses you use not to share your faith stories?

How could you use your spiritual gifts to demonstrate God's love and open doors for spiritual conversations?

How do your non-Christian friends know that you are a Christ-follower?

Become a Storyteller

I'm a work in progress. I don't tell my stories as well or as consistently as I'd like. So if you feel inept or stumble over your words from time to time, join the club. Tell your stories anyway. I am convinced that God can use our sincere efforts to bring glory to Himself. As Bill Fay, author of *Share Jesus without Fear* says, "God can use anything you say. The only thing He can't use is your silence."

Our blog, CaseysOnMission.com, serves as one way for us to share what God is doing in our lives, as well as a tool for staying connected to people who have committed to praying for our work in Ireland. We chose the name, Caseys on Mission, as a *reminder to ourselves* about our purpose wherever we live. *On mission* isn't a designation or title. In fact, we very rarely use the word *missionary* to describe our role here. Yes, we are part of a church-planting team, but when someone I meet asks what I do, or why I'm in Ireland, my response is, "I'm a writer and editor, and I'm volunteering with a church to help people learn about Jesus and the Bible." If I'm on my toes, I might add something like, "we talk with people about a Biblical alternative to religion."

The truth is, all Christians are "on mission." We all have a role to play. We all have faith stories to share.

My desire with this book and the study I did to write it, is simply to challenge and equip people (myself included) to talk freely, honestly, and naturally about how our lives are different because of Jesus. My prayer is that you will become intentional about noticing and sharing how God is at work in your life.

I'd love to hear your story.

Get Personal

Share your story with me!
Visit **ShareYourFaithStory.net** and use the "share" link to tell me your story.

Keep a journal.
If you don't already, start keeping a journal to help you notice and remember how God shows up in your life. Go to ShareYourFaithStory.net to get your free *Get Personal Story Journal.*

Start saying Jesus's name in daily conversation.
The more we talk about spiritual things, the more natural it feels. Giving God credit for the beauty of a sunset is a simple way to start. If Jesus's peace is the only way you're surviving today's craziness, say so—no matter who's listening.

Pray for wisdom and courage.
Ask the Holy Spirit to help you recognize and make the most of opportunities to share your faith stories.

About the Author

Erin K. Casey is a wife, mom, writer, and photographer. She's also the author of a children's adventure series: *Zany Zia's Hats to Where*. Through her stories and images, she hopes to inspire people to see God at work in their lives.

As a ghostwriter, editor, and book coach, she has helped bestselling authors as well as business and life coaches share their messages effectively and professionally. She has written articles on topics ranging from faith and religion, to entrepreneurship, as well as celebrity and business profiles. Her work has been featured in *SUCCESS Magazine*, *Empowering Women*, *Live Happy*, and *Success from Home* among others.

In 2013, Erin and her husband, Brian, joined a church-planting team in Ireland. Learn more at ErinKCasey.com and CaseysOnMisson.com.

CPSIA information can be obtained
at www.ICGtesting.com
Printed in the USA
LVOW01s0743021115
460701LV00003B/8/P